Performing Arts Handbook

Grade 4

Printed in the United States of America

ISBN 0-15-309765-5

2 3 4 5 6 7 8 9 10 073 2000 99 98

Harcourt Brace & Company

Orlando Atlanta Austin Boston San Francisco Chicago Dallas New York Toronto London

http://www.hbschool.com

Contents

UNIT 1

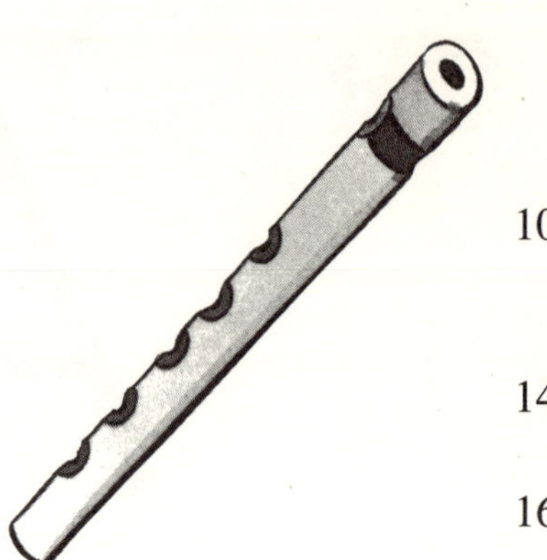

UNIT 2

UNIT 3

UNIT 4

UNIT 5

UNIT 6

RESOURCES

Performing Arts Activities Enrich Visual Arts Instruction

SETTING: *Mrs. J.'s third-grade class is looking at Renoir's* Girl with a Watering Can *for the second time this week. During the instruction, the teacher guides the discussion with questions and ideas, preparing her students for a performing arts activity.*

MRS. J.: What is the girl in the painting doing?

MONICA: Watering the flowers.

ALEX: Maybe she is all done with the watering can.

MRS. J.: That could be. Philipé, this week you are watering the plants in our classroom. Could you show us how you do it? *(Philipé demonstrates with a watering can and the plants.)* Great. Do you think you could show us how to do that **without** the watering can? Could you pantomime that for us? *(Philipé pantomimes the action.)* Alex, Josh, and Amy, why don't you join Philipé and pantomime this action for us.

Applying Performing Arts to Visual Arts Instruction

While Mrs. J.'s students have benefited from earlier discussions about *Girl with a Watering Can,* they are beginning to explore creative ways to respond to it using the performing arts. Children are naturally drawn to music, movement, and drama, and many learn best (in any and all content areas) when they can express themselves using the media of music, dance, and/or theater. Additionally, students may approach the kinesthetic and aural performing arts activities with self-confidence that may be lacking when they attempt to create (visual) art.

In the scene on page 4 Mrs. J. shows how to involve her students in the discussion preceeding an activity. She knows that Philipé, who is an ESL student, will be successful with his pantomime. Later on she may have him explain what he did in his pantomime, helping him develop his oral language skills. Alex learns best with kinesthetic activities, so Mrs. J. quickly draws him into the pantomime. Whether Mrs. J. chooses to do the activity with the whole class or small groups, she can use the *Performing Arts Handbook* to develop discussions about art and cultivate students' creative responses.

Using the *Performing Arts Handbook*

The *Performing Arts Handbook* offers two strands of instructional support for ART EXPRESS.

- Unit projects expand on the program unit ideas about the visual arts. A four- to six-week performing arts project culminates in a performance such as a circus, a play, a concert, or a dance. Although the focus of the performing arts project is the performance, students are encouraged to develop their talents and skills (with specific goals for creative expression, artistic perception, historical/cultural context, and aesthetic valuing) during the process. (See pages 6–9 for ideas on how to assess students and manage the classroom during these projects.)
- *Art Print* activities (such as the one Mrs. J. used) provide an opportunity to extend the learning and appreciation of fine art by drawing students into a performing arts response. With these 30–40-minute lessons, students interact with the painting through their imaginations. Suggestions for dance, music, and theater responses are offered for each *Art Print*.

Learning about the visual arts can expand students' interests and creative abilities. Integrating visual and performing arts is a natural way to "grab" student interest. There is no better way to discover students' potential to learn and have fun at the same time!

Also available—

Performing Arts Cassettes

Grades 1–2* and *Grades 3–5

●

For each *Art Print* activity, a music selection from the *Performing Arts Cassette: Grades 3–5* is cited.

Using Project Journals to Manage the Classroom and Assess Students

What is a PROJECT JOURNAL?

Classroom journals can be created and used for all kinds of purposes—to explore concepts learned in math, reading, and science, for example. A project journal is another kind of record that documents the work and the process of a long-term project for a group or an individual student.

If the whole class is collaborating on a single unit project, such as a play or a concert, one journal would be kept for the class. Small groups working on a project would each keep a group journal. A student working independently on a project would keep an individual journal.

Students compile and organize materials in a three-ring binder. The binder becomes a chronological record of all work done by group members.

The journal has several purposes. Students can use it to keep track of their own work on the unit project over the course of several weeks. The teacher benefits from the record of work showing the progress made. The journal is the touchpoint for everyone connected with the project. When group members meet and make decisions, they add to the binder. Students can return to the binder during appropriate work times to check on group and individual work, even if other group members are not present.

What do students write and keep in the binder during the course of the project?

Meeting notes, plans, sketches, lists, research notes, handouts, and records of setbacks are just some of the things students keep in their project journals. Assessment copying masters (such as the ones on pages 58 and 59) may also be filled out and put in the binder. Encourage students to be creative and concerned about keeping the journal up to date.

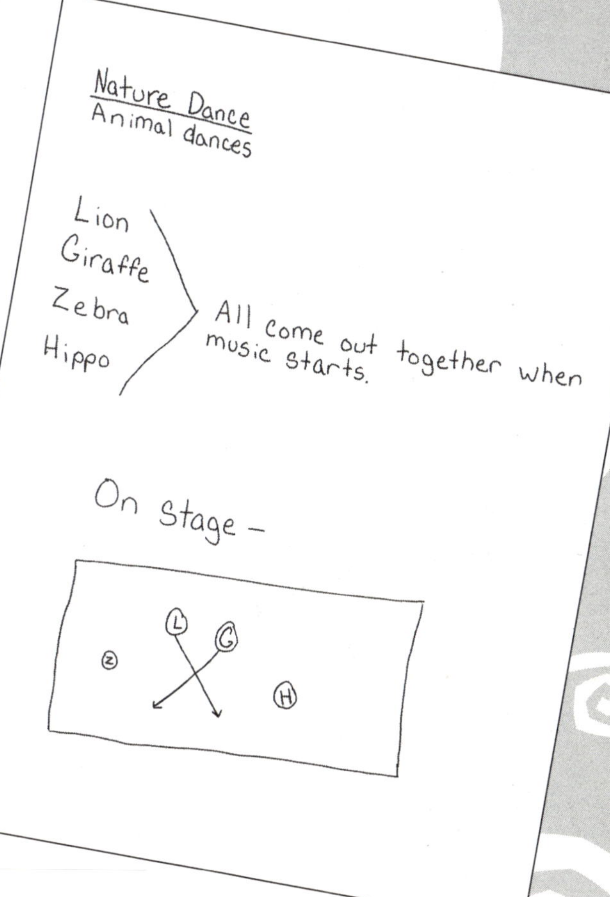

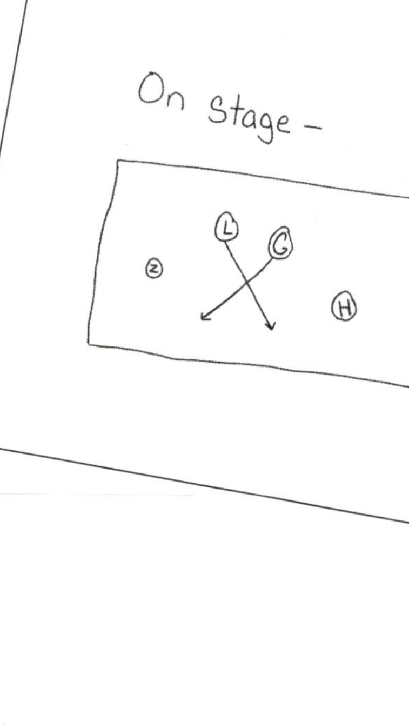

How does the project journal assist with classroom management and assessment?

Once students have an understanding of the project goals, they can begin to plan their project using the goals as a guide and the project journal as a means to organize tasks and keep track of progress.

The project journal gives group members

- the opportunity to involve all group members in making decisions that concern the final performance.
- the ability to organize, plan, and record each step of the process, including changes.
- project-related information for peer and self-assessments.

The project journal allows teachers

- to assess students' individual and group efforts, organization, planning, and execution of work as part of the final performance.
- to put decision-making in the hands of students.

The project *process* (recorded in the project journal) is an important part of the final product—the performance.

Look!
Music Rehearsal for all musicians will be during Music Class on Thursday.
Actors and crew will stay in class to rehearse with me.
Mrs. Davis

Cast

Benjamin Banneker-
Benjamin Franklin-
Mrs. Morris-Miranda
shopkeeper #1-Brittany
shopkeeper #2-

Crew
music-Michael H.
props-Veronica
instuments-Alex and Veronica
costumes-Mrs. Kuklinski

Tell me more about how the project journal can help students meet individual needs. What about students with special needs?

The opportunity to set project goals and to make choices about how to meet those goals invites students to match the tasks that need to be accomplished with the talents of the group members. Students who prefer not to perform can still take on meaningful tasks. Unit Project lessons guide students as they choose roles and tasks. Recording their responsibilities in the binder makes all group members feel involved and important.

Students with special needs also have special talents. Whether or not they choose to perform, they can participate in group roles that develop and enhance their interaction with group members and build their sense of self-worth. Defining and clarifying group member roles in the project journal—sometimes two or three times during the course of a project—allows all students to identify their part in the group effort.

Nature Dance

Unit Project Overview: As students study relationships between art and the natural world, they create a dance performance that conveys concepts about nature.

MATERIALS

- *Performing Arts Cassette* or recordings of Native American and nature music
- simple rhythm instruments
- materials for simple costumes and props
- videotape: *Swan Lake* (Philips Classics, 1966)

VOCABULARY CONCEPTS

You may wish to teach these **Glossary** words and concepts in context during the project.

choreographer
choreography
rhythm
tempo

CROSS-CURRICULAR CONNECTIONS

Fine Arts Dance, Music
Science Environment, Habitats, Landforms, Plants, Animals
Social Studies Geography, Cultural Traditions, Feelings

PROJECT OBJECTIVES

Artistic Perception Choose and perform dance movements and describe how the movements feel, using the language of dance.

Creative Expression Create rhythmic patterns of movement based on rhythms and movements observed in nature.

Historical/Cultural Context View a videotape of a traditional dance that represents something in nature.

Aesthetic Valuing Discuss the differences between the dances developed by the groups, with an emphasis on how dance elements were used by each group.

1 WARM-UP

Choose one of the following activities:

- Invite volunteers to choose an animal and to pantomime, with or without music, how it moves. The others can guess what animal is being portrayed. Encourage the whole group to move like animals. Discuss how the movements remind students of real animals. Ask how they might use movement to show something about the natural world.
- Have students view a live or videotaped dance performance with a nature theme, such as *Swan Lake* or a traditional Native American dance. Discuss how the dancers' movements suggest elements of nature, and invite students to share ideas for a dance they could create to show part of nature.

Have students discuss the following questions and record responses in their project journals:

- **Which animal would you like to portray?**
- **How can you use movement to show something from nature?**

❷ PLAN THE PROJECT

Set Goals Assist students with the following goals:

- create, learn, and perform a dance sequence
- dance with a group, synchronizing moves
- produce a cohesive, meaningful performance

Outline the Project With students, consider the following:

- the scope of the project (see Project Options)
- the audience—such as families or younger students
- which ecosystem the class will focus on and what features of it small groups will portray
- research needed: animals, plants, geography, customs and traditional dances of indigenous people

Once small groups have been organized, students should begin identifying and defining tasks for their group. All group work can be recorded in separate sections of the project journal.

❸ EXPLORE DANCE IDEAS

- Group members choose individual roles for the project, such as Leader, Dance Captain, Music Director, and Writer.
- Students choose music to accompany their dances. They may want to experiment with different kinds of music and rhythm instruments.
- Students experiment with different movements and tempos, and then discuss how each conveys a different message.

PROJECT OPTIONS

- Without costumes, props, or sets, students can create and perform dances to music for classmates. **SIMPLE**
- Students can develop stories for their dances. After students write scripts and choreograph the dances, the final performance, with costumes and sets, could be part of a cultural or an environmental celebration. **ELABORATE**

Contact parents and local dance schools to find dancers or choreographers who can coach students or demonstrate dances.

4 CREATE A DANCE

- As students invent their dances, encourage them to teach each other and provide feedback to group members.
- Using the Copying Master on page 13 as a guide for notating movements, students can record dance steps.
- Students should decide on any costumes they want to use and begin making them.

CLASSROOM MANAGEMENT
Before dress rehearsals, have each group make a checklist of day-of-the-performance tasks and assignments.

5 REHEARSE AND REFINE

- Students rehearse their performances, with all groups performing their dances in order.
- Have at least one dress rehearsal.
- Students who are not performing may help coordinate the groups' dances and audio needs, make and deliver invitations, and create the program for the performance.

For Students with Special Needs
Students who use wheelchairs can coordinate their movements with those of other students. Encourage group members to work together to include wheelchair movements in their choreography.

6 PERFORM IT!

Some options for the performance:
- videotape the performance so that it can be shared with family members or the community outside of school
- set up a stage setting and an audience space outdoors

Performance and Process Assessments

Encourage students to add personal evaluations and responses about the performance to the project journal.

✔ For the Student
- What part of nature do you think your dance showed best? Why was it effective?
- How did the audience respond to your performance?

✔ For the Teacher
- How effectively did students convey elements of the ecosystem?
- How were plans and group interactions indicative of the final performance?

CAREERS IN ART

Students should be aware of these dance-related careers as they work on this project.

choreographer
conductor
dancer
director
musician

Name ______________________________

PERFORMING ARTS PROJECT

Nature Dance

Learning About Dance Notations

When a **choreographer** creates a new dance, he or she creates all the movements for dancers. Leg, arm, hand, and body movements are carefully planned for a performance. Then the **choreography** is recorded in writing called dance notations. The dance notations help the choreographer remember the movements and teach them to dancers.

Dance notations can be made in different ways. You can write them out. You can draw them and write labels. Or you can invent a combination of words, symbols, and pictures like the ones below.

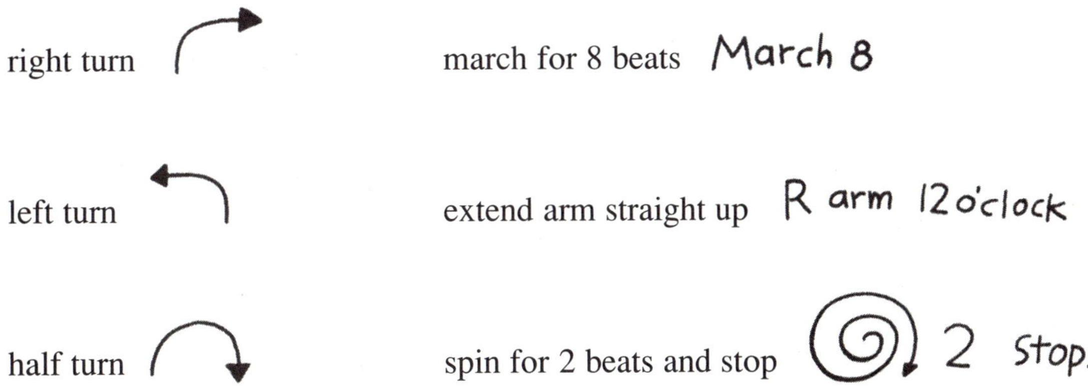

Whatever style you choose for your dance notations, be sure to write out detailed directions so you don't forget the choreography.

A Dialogue: "At Home with . . ."

▲ ***Art Print 1,*** *Hunt's Vase,* Janet Fish

OBJECTIVE: Students prepare and perform a dialogue around a character.

MATERIALS: *Art Print 1, Performing Arts Cassette*: "Salut d'Amour, Op. 12"

TIPS AND TIME-SAVERS Suggest that group members concentrate on their characters and think of broad ideas for the dialogue. They can improvise the actual dialogue when the group presents to classmates.

WARM-UP

Display *Art Print 1*, the still life *Hunt's Vase*, as you play "Salut d'Amour, Op. 12." Ask volunteers to describe what they see. Encourage students to share what they notice about the lines, colors, and use of reflection in the painting, and the mood the painting creates. Discuss the following:

- **What objects are displayed on the table?**
- **What do the objects suggest about the person who arranged them? What kind of person would put these objects together?**
- **What is important to the person who arranged the objects? How can you tell?**

THEATER ACTIVITY

Have students form small groups of four or five, and explain that each group will create characters and a dialogue based on the objects on the table. One student can act as the owner of the table, and the other students are company who are visiting that person for the first time. The dialogue should be about the objects on the table and the way they are arranged. Encourage students to think about some of the following questions as they develop their dialogues:

- **Who is the owner of the objects? Where does the person live?**
- **What does the rest of the room look like?**
- **What friends would the person have? Who might be visiting?**
- **Is there a specific reason for the visit? What might guests ask or say about the objects on the table?**
- **What interesting stories can you make up about the objects on the table?**

Allow time for groups to develop short dialogues. Invite groups to perform their dialogues for the rest of the class. As groups present their dialogues, encourage classmates to take notes about each performance for reference during whole-group discussion.

REFLECT

Have students look again at *Hunt's Vase*. Ask them to share new insights about the painting that the performances may have brought to mind. Encourage discussion about the process of creating characters based on objects pictured in a still life. You may also wish to discuss the following questions:

- **Did working on the dialogue help you feel differently about the painting? If so, how?**
- **What parts of the performances helped make you feel closer to the painting or to the artist?**

Informal Assessment

✔ Were students' characters convincing?

✔ How well did the dialogues touch on elements in the painting?

MUSICAL PARTS **Have students create musical sounds for the four main sets of objects in the painting. They can arrange these sounds in a way that echoes how the objects are arranged in the painting. ■ GOAL: CREATIVE EXPRESSION**

DANCING ON AIR **Ask students to focus on the creatures at the base of the vase or else on the flower petals. Have them choose music (or use "The Dance of the Sugarplum Fairy" from Tchaikovsky's *Nutcracker Suite*), and then create movements that show how the creatures might move through air, or how the petals might move as they fall to the table. ■ GOAL: ARTISTIC PERCEPTION**

MUSIC AESTHETIC VALUING

Music for a Meal

▲ ***Art Print 2,*** *Still Life*, Floris van Dyck

OBJECTIVE: Students choose music that complements an artwork and justify their choices.

MATERIALS: *Art Print 2, Performing Arts Cassette*: "Bergerie" and other musical recordings (optional)

CLASSROOM MANAGEMENT

Students may find it helpful to make a sign-up sheet to schedule times for listening to the *Performing Arts Cassette* and other recordings. Due to the time needed for listening before making a choice, it may be more efficient for students to complete this activity in small groups.

WARM-UP

Display *Art Print 2, Still Life,* and mention that it was painted about 400 years ago. Ask students to look closely at the print for clues it gives about the time of year, the relative well-being of the owners of the table, and about life in general during that time period. Discuss any of the following questions:

- **What does this painting make you think about?**
- **What objects in the painting give clues about the time of year?**
- **Do you think the table is set for a meal? What meal might it be? Do you think anyone has eaten already?**
- **Look at the things in the painting that are not food. What do these things suggest about the people who owned them?**
- **How is the meal in the painting different from a meal that you might eat? How is it the same?**

MUSIC ACTIVITY

Explain to students that they will be listening to and choosing musical selections that they think complement *Art Print 2*. They might choose music created during the same time as the painting, or select pieces that have a mood like that in the painting. Point out to students that they will share their choices with classmates and explain why they feel the selections fit the painting.

- Encourage students to think about questions like the following as they listen to the *Performing Arts Cassette* or other musical recordings.
  - **What would you listen to as you ate this meal?**
  - **What feelings or ideas does the painting suggest to you? What music can you find that gives you similar feelings or ideas?**

- Allow time for students to listen and make their selections. Remind them that there are no "right" or "wrong" choices that they can make, but that they will have to give reasons for the choices they make.
- Play "Bergerie," and ask students how well they think this piece fits the painting. Encourage students who selected this piece to share their reasons for choosing it.
- Have students share the music they selected and explain why they chose it. If other students chose the same piece, have them add their reasons for selecting it. Encourage the rest of the group to analyze each selection and discuss how well it fits the painting.

REFLECT

Have students look again at *Art Print 2,* and discuss the following questions:

- **Did any of the musical selections surprise you? In what ways?**
- **How did the different pieces of music change the way you looked at the painting?**

Informal Assessment

✔ Were students able to relate the mood of a piece of music to the mood of the painting?

✔ How well were students able to justify the music they selected?

HISTORICAL SKITS Students may research family life in early-seventeenth-century Europe. When students have gained some insight into the time period, small groups can develop historical skits that show some aspect of family life they have discovered. ■ GOAL: HISTORICAL/CULTURAL CONTEXT

OBJECTS IN MOTION
Students can study the objects in the painting and develop movements for them. They can figure out ways to move like the curled apple peel, the bowl of apples, the plate of grapes, the knife, or a hunk of cheese. They could then perform (with or without music) for classmates, who will guess which parts of the painting the dancers are representing. ■ GOAL: ARTISTIC PERCEPTION

Monologues in Character

Unit Project Overview: While studying how visual artists portray different aspects of people, students create a monologue for a character.

MATERIALS

- *Performing Arts Cassette* or other musical recordings
- materials for simple costumes and props

VOCABULARY CONCEPTS

You may wish to teach these **Glossary** words and concepts in context during the project.

character
improvisation
monologue
role

CROSS-CURRICULAR CONNECTIONS

Fine Arts Dance
Social Studies
Contemporary Culture, Feelings, Observing People

PROJECT OBJECTIVES

Artistic Perception Move, speak, and act like person students have observed.

Creative Expression Convey the emotions and emotional qualities of a character through dramatization.

Historical/Cultural Context Represent various cultures and languages in monologues, depending upon the character students create monologues about.

Aesthetic Valuing Discuss the success of one another's characterizations.

1 WARM-UP

Choose one of the following activities to help students begin thinking about developing characters:

- Have each student observe someone (preferably someone that the class does not know) and study the way that person moves, walks, and talks. As a student describes a person, other students listen to the description and try to move, walk, and talk like the person being described.
- Have students think of well-known characters from television, books, or film, or famous performers or sports figures. Volunteers act like their character in some way, imitating movements, saying favorite phrases, and so on. Other students can guess the character and discuss how they could identify him or her.

Have students discuss the following questions and record responses in individual project journals:

- **What is important to remember when you're trying to create a character?**
- **How does trying to impersonate someone change the way you think about that person?**

❷ PLAN THE PROJECT

Set Goals Assist students with the following project goals:

- observe and note characteristics of another person
- write and perform a monologue about a character
- attempt to show, rather than tell, what the character is like

Outline the Project As students develop their ideas about the project, consider:

- the scope of the project (see Project Options)
- the audience—such as fellow classmates or family members
- how many minutes (2-4) to allow for each monologue
- the performance schedule for the monologues

Students may need time to create a subject for their monologues. Remind them that everyone is unique and worthy of respect, regardless of ways they may be different from others. Point out that actors try to identify with and feel what their characters feel. Have students use individual project journals to record their thoughts about monologue subjects.

❸ EXPLORE THE CHARACTER

Suggest that students use the Character Web (Copying Master, page 21) as a guide to develop their characters. Have them also consider the following:

- What words come to mind when you think about this character?
- What does the character like and dislike?
- How does the character act in different situations? What does he or she say and do when happy, sad, anxious, pleased, excited?

PROJECT OPTIONS

- Students perform their completed monologues for the class, a few at a time over a period of days. **SIMPLE**
- Students create a videotaped montage of the characters they have created with their monologues and share it with other classes, family members, and other interested viewers. **ELABORATE**

CONNECTION

Encourage interested parents or members of a local theater company to share their impressions of the characters and the parts of their personalities that make them so memorable. If actors visit the class, have them demonstrate things they do to "get into character" when they prepare for a performance.

CLASSROOM MANAGEMENT
When students are ready to share their monologues in small groups, you may want to have them practice quietly in a hallway.

For Students with Special Needs
Visually-impaired students will have to limit their characterizations to vocal tone and perhaps gestures. The concept of character may be too abstract for some mentally challenged students. It may be more realistic to ask them to do impressions of people they know well.

CAREERS IN ART

Students should be aware of these theater-related careers as they work on this project.

actor
comedian
playwright/scriptwriter
director
costume designer

4 CREATE A MONOLOGUE

As students begin to write monologues, they might find these suggestions helpful as they develop their characters.

- Use simple costumes or props.
- Think of activities that you could pantomime while you speak.
- Gestures, favorite sayings, and vocal tone enrich the characterization.

5 REHEARSE AND REFINE

- Students should decide whether they will read or memorize their monologues.
- Students can share their monologues with small groups. During discussions group members talk about presentations.
- The whole group may wish to discuss the different monologues and organize the presentations, grouping monologues that go together and taking timing into account.

6 PERFORM IT!

Some options for the performance:

- a week-long performance series, with students performing a few at a time each day
- videotape the monologues and lend the tape to other classes, family members, or community groups

Performance and Process Assessments

Review with students the project journals and their performances based on the goals set at the beginning of the project. Encourage students to add personal evaluations and responses to the project journals.

✔ For the Student

- What was the easiest part of your character to recreate? What was the hardest? Why?
- If you based your character on a real person, what would that person say about your performance?

✔ For the Teacher

- How well did students portray the character?
- Were students able to speak and move like the character during the whole monologue?

Name ____________________

PERFORMING ARTS PROJECT

Monologues in Character

Character Web

Says Things Like:

____

____

____

Favorite Things:

____

____

____

Talks Like:

____

____

____

____

Character's Name

Least Favorite Things:

____

____

____

Other Characteristics:

____

____

____

Moves Like:

____

____

____

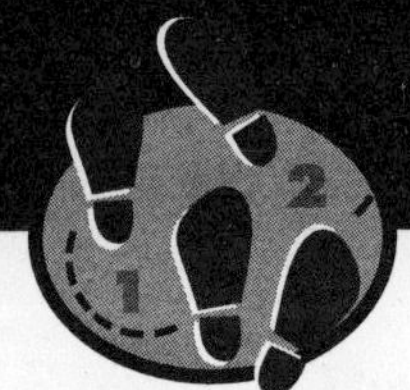

Dinner Dance

▲ ***Art Print 3,*** *The Gourmet,* Pablo Picasso

OBJECTIVE: Students create, critique, and analyze dance movements.

MATERIALS: *Art Print 3, Performing Arts Cassette:* "Rondeau from Suite No. 2 in B minor," cooking utensils to use as props (if desired)

TIPS AND TIME-SAVERS Some students may be more comfortable sharing their improvisations with small groups rather than with the whole class.

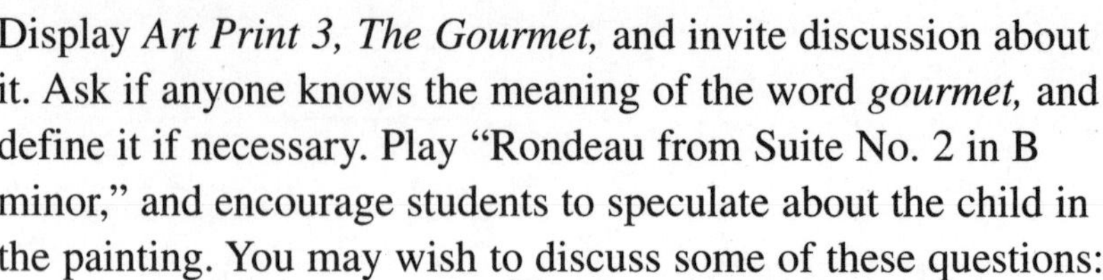

WARM-UP

Display *Art Print 3, The Gourmet,* and invite discussion about it. Ask if anyone knows the meaning of the word *gourmet,* and define it if necessary. Play "Rondeau from Suite No. 2 in B minor," and encourage students to speculate about the child in the painting. You may wish to discuss some of these questions:

- **Do you think the child is a boy or a girl? Why?**
- **How does the painting make you feel? Why do you think so?**
- **Why do you think Picasso named this painting *The Gourmet*?**

DANCE ACTIVITY

Tell students that they will be creating dance moves that have something to do with cooking or eating.

- Have students pantomime movements that they use when cooking or eating. Remind them that dance movements take place on a larger scale than the movements we make while going about our daily activities.
- Students may continue working on their moves alone, with a partner, or in a small group. Suggest they think about the following points:
  - **How does a hungry person eat? How is this different from the way someone who is full eats?**
  - **How can you use your whole body to show how someone cooks or eats?**
  - **For those working in groups, what movements can each person make to show someone cooking or a group of people eating?**
- Have students choose music to accompany their dances, if they wish.

- When students have had a bit more time to develop their dance moves, ask volunteers to share their dance sequences with the class. Ask students watching classmates perform to analyze and give feedback about the effectiveness of the movements according to some of the following points:
  - How well did the dancer(s) use space?
  - Did dancers working in groups coordinate moves with each other?
  - How creative were dancers in making up their dance moves?

REFLECT

Return to *The Gourmet* and discuss students' reactions to translating everyday actions into dance movements. Ask:

- **Did the dance movements that you did or watched help you appreciate *The Gourmet*? Explain.**
- **What new thoughts about the painting do you have now that you have performed or watched a performance?**

Informal Assessment

✔ Did students use movement that was relevant?

✔ If students used music, how well did their movements go with the music? How did the music add to their performances?

✔ Did students' analysis of the different dance sequences show an understanding of the activity?

IMPROV AT THE TABLE In small groups, students improvise a dinner (or meal preparation), using as props the objects seen in the painting: bowl, spoon, cup, table, cloth. Students develop dialogue and use gestures as they build a scene around the props at hand.

■ **GOAL: CREATIVE EXPRESSION**

A MOOD PIECE Students study the painting. Keeping the mood of the painting in mind, students create or find a piece of music that has a similar mood. Students share their compositions or the pieces they find with classmates and discuss how looking at the painting while listening to different pieces of music makes them see the painting differently.

■ **GOAL: ARTISTIC PERCEPTION**

MUSIC CREATIVE EXPRESSION

Colorful Music Creations

▲ ***Art Print 4,*** *The Boating Party,* Mary Cassatt

OBJECTIVE: Students create sounds that represent color.

MATERIALS: *Art Print 4, Performing Arts Cassette:* "Arabesque #1 in E major," other music by Claude Debussy such as *Debussy by the Sea* (Special Music Co. 4723 4962 2), found objects (see Tips and Time-Savers)

TIPS AND TIME-SAVERS Start a box of found objects for music activities. Include materials such as jars of sand, nuts, bolts, nails, keys, buttons, rice, sheets of sandpaper, wood, sticks, combs, containers, and so on.

WARM-UP

To help re-create the sounds of calm water, speak in a soft voice and play "Arabesque #1 in E major" by Claude Debussy. Display *The Boating Party* and ask volunteers to describe the scene and the characters in the painting. Discuss any of the following:

- **Where do you think these characters are going?**
- **What is the mood of the characters in the painting?**
- **What do the colors in the painting tell you about the mood?**

MUSIC ACTIVITY

- Explain to students that Debussy wrote his music around the same time that Cassatt and other Impressionist artists did their work. Debussy was interested in the colorful images he could create with his music.
- Have students work in pairs to create musical sounds based upon color. When pairs have chosen a color they would like to work with, provide found objects and ordinary materials for them to explore. Encourage them to reflect and think creatively as you ask the following questions:

  What is your color? Where is it found in nature?

  What does your color sound like to you?

- Then have students experiment with the colors and sounds. Invite them to share the sounds with other pairs. If several pairs have worked on the same color, such as blue, have them compare the sounds they created. Ask them to be specific about the color blue.

  Find an example of the color blue you created. Is it dark or light? How does your music show the color?

  Does your sound for the color blue match the color blue in *The Boating Party?*

REFLECT

Gather students together to look again at *The Boating Party*. Play "Arabesque #1 in E major" and have students study the colors in the painting as they listen. Then discuss the following:

- **What do the colors tell you about Cassatt and the way she looked at things?**
- **Which colors tell you about the mood of the painting?**
- **What does Debussy's music add to the painting?**

Informal Assessment

✔ How did students integrate the concepts of color and sound?

✔ What were students able to extrapolate from the painting and the music?

MEET THE ARTISTS

What if Mary Cassatt and Claude Debussy met? After students have examined *The Boating Party* and listened to "Arabesque #1 in E major," have them write a list of questions that Cassatt and Debussy might have for each other. Have pairs of students take turns role-playing the artists. ■ GOAL: ARTISTIC PERCEPTION

DANCING COLORS

Spread on the floor a mural-sized sheet of paper. First have students dance (without shoes) on the paper as they listen to the music of Debussy. Then have students paint the paper with watercolors using various sizes of brushes or sponges. Encourage them to use colors and lines that represent the dance they first did. ■ GOAL: CREATIVE EXPRESSION

Musical Collages

Unit Project Overview: As students study how artists express their unique viewpoints, small groups work together to compile and/or create musical collages.

MATERIALS

- *Performing Arts Cassette* and/or other recordings
- rhythm instruments
- picture sources such as old magazines, newspapers (optional)
- art materials (optional)

VOCABULARY CONCEPTS

You may wish to teach these **Glossary** words and concepts in context during the project.

expression
music types (Baroque, classical, jazz, pop/rock, etc.)
notation

CROSS-CURRICULAR CONNECTIONS

Fine Arts Theater, Dance, Visual Art
Science Sound, Natural Environments
Social Studies Cultural Traditions, History, Human Environments, Feelings
Math Measuring Time

PROJECT OBJECTIVES

Artistic Perception Explore a variety of music types and describe the feelings, ideas, and impressions evoked.

Creative Expression Choose a group of musical selections that express certain feelings, ideas, and impressions about a topic. Create an original composition.

Historical/Cultural Context Listen and respond to music from diverse cultures.

Aesthetic Valuing Decide which musical selections express an aspect of a topic. Present selections in a creative arrangement to share ideas, feelings, and impressions.

1 WARM-UP

Choose one of the following activities:

- Play a selection from the *Performing Arts Cassette.* Ask students to imagine a person, place, or thing that the selection reminds them of. Encourage volunteers to describe their impressions in detail. Play other selections from the *Performing Arts Cassette* and discuss what they remind students of. Lead students to conclude that music can evoke a variety of feelings, moods, and impressions.
- Ask volunteers to bring in recordings of their favorite music to share with the class. As individuals present their choices, discuss why they like the particular selection and how it makes them feel.

Have students discuss the following questions and record responses in their project journals.

- **Think of your favorite pieces of music. How does the music make you feel? What does it make you think of?**
- **Think of some music you dislike. When you hear this music, what does it make you think of?**

❷ PLAN THE PROJECT

Set Goals Explain to students that they will be exploring the relationship between music and feelings. Assist them with the following project goals:

- listen to a variety of music selections and types
- choose diverse selections to form musical collages that evoke impressions of persons, places, or things
- create original compositions to include in the collages

Outline the Project With students, consider the following:

- the scope of the project (see Project Options)
- the audience: Family members? Other classes?
- research needed: How can we decide on the topic? Where can we find the music? From personal/family music collections? From the library? From other sources?

Small groups should be formed based on interest. Possible topics might include subjects as varied as "the ocean," "happiness," "friendship," "the city." Students might choose topics based on what they are studying in other curriculum areas.

❸ EXPLORE TOPICS AND MUSIC

- Groups should brainstorm topics and vote on one to explore in depth. This might be accomplished by listening to selections from the *Performing Arts Cassette* and discussing what feelings and ideas various selections evoke.
- Once a topic has been chosen, group members should start exploring and choosing musical selections that express their ideas and feelings. Encourage them to explore and include different types of music; for example, if students choose to explore the sea, they might include "Le Mer" by Debussy (classical), "Surfin' USA" by the Beach Boys (popular/rock), "My Bonnie Lies over the Ocean" (traditional/folk).
- Encourage each group to create an original composition.

PROJECT OPTIONS

- Each group can compile and arrange three to five audiotaped selections representing various music types. Groups might work on several different topics over the course of the project and present their musical collages to classmates for discussion. **SIMPLE**
- Each group can create a music video, including visual as well as aural expressions of their topic. Students can collect and/or create pictures to display as selections are played. **ELABORATE**

CONNECTION

Inform family members, local libraries, and community groups of project goals. Enlist their help in providing a wide range of recordings.

CLASSROOM MANAGEMENT
Have each group choose a "technology manager" who will operate recorders and keep track of cassettes. If necessary, tutor these students in using the available equipment.

For Students with Special Needs
All students should be able to participate in this project. For example, hearing-impaired students can often relate and respond to music by feeling the vibrations as music is played. Encourage and help each small group to accommodate the needs of all members.

CAREERS IN ART

Students should be aware of these music-related careers as they work on this project.

- **musician**
- **composer**
- **recording technician**
- **conductor**
- **arranger**

4 CREATE MUSICAL COLLAGES

- As students choose selections, help them consider the following: How should we order the selections to represent the topic? Should we tape or perform original compositions? Should we videotape our collage and include visual images and/or creative movements?
- Use the Copying Master on page 29 to help students record melodies for original compositions.
- Visual presentations should be finalized. Costumes and scenery should be planned and created at this time.

5 REHEARSE AND REFINE

- Spend time with each group, listening to the music they have chosen. Discuss what they want to tell about their topic and how the selections express their ideas.
- Have each group present their collage to another group. The listeners can provide feedback about how well the presenters have accomplished their goals.

6 PERFORM IT!

Some options for the performance:
- videotape presentations, including responses and discussion, to share with family members and other classes
- have groups present their collages to each other and other classes, and then discuss responses and impressions

Performance and Process Assessments

Review the project with students by discussing their project journal entries and their presentations. Encourage students to record their feelings about the project in their project journals.

✔ For the Student
- What did you learn about music during this project?
- Did you discover that you like music that you may or may not have heard before? What new types of music did you discover?

✔ For the Teacher
- How effective were students in expressing their ideas and feelings about a topic through music?
- How did students work cooperatively to create a cohesive presentation that incorporated their individual ideas and feelings?

Name ______________________________

PERFORMING ARTS PROJECT

Musical Collages

Remembering Music You Write

When composers create music, they use special symbols to write down the musical notes. It takes a lot of study to learn this music language.

What if you don't know this music language? How can you remember music you create? You can draw it! There are two important things to show in your drawing:

- how the notes go up and down
- if the notes are long or short

Here is an example from the song "Home on the Range."

Instead of large and small bars, you could use circles, squares, stars, or some other shape. You could even use money. A small coin could stand for a short note, and a large coin could stand for a long note.

THEATER HISTORICAL AND CULTURAL CONTEXT

Portrait of Farm Life

▲ ***Art Print 5,*** *Sodbuster: San Isidro*, Luis Jiménez

OBJECTIVE: Students act out a scene based on farmwork of the past.

MATERIALS: *Art Print 5, Performing Arts Cassette:* "Fanfare for the Common Man"

CLASSROOM MANAGEMENT Give students two or three minutes to talk over plans for their improvisations. Some improvisations may need your guidance, especially the first ones. Side-coaching about movements, expressions, and details is a helpful technique to use.

WARM-UP

Play "Fanfare for the Common Man" as students view *Sodbuster: San Isidro*. Ask volunteers to describe what they see. Discuss any of the following:

- **What is a sodbuster?**
- **In terms of United States geography, where do you think this sculpture is located?**
- **What message do you think the artist gave to viewers with this sculpture?**

THEATER ACTIVITY

- Discuss people who work on a farm, such as family members, hired hands, and seasonal workers. Have students become some of these characters. Ask students to suggest possible situations for improvisation; for example, they could improvise scenes between a father and son who have specific work to get done, the farmer and his wife discussing food preparations, or a conversation between a farmer and seasonal workers who will harvest a crop. Then have them present their improvisations.

- Organize students into small groups. Explain that each group will create a scene showing some farmwork. To provide variety to the performances, have groups choose different tasks with different tools involved. Encourage students to emphasize the movements and physical action of the work.

- Have student groups make a chart that lists the manual labor of farmwork. Also, they should list the tools or skills needed to do this job. For example:

WORK	TOOLS
plowing by hand	plow, oxen

Have students present their scenes and then discuss what they liked or disliked about their performances. Ask them to tell or write what they might change if they replayed the scene.

REFLECT

Gather students in front of *Sodbuster: San Isidro*. Play "Fanfare for the Common Man" again as students study the picture. Then discuss the following questions:

- **What can you tell about the life of the man in the sculpture?**
- **Where do you see power in the sculpture?**
- **Are there any other jobs we do today that are like the hard work of the farmer? What are they?**

Informal Assessment

✔ Were students able to improvise the characters with their body movements as well as with dialogue?

✔ How well did students describe the movement and drama of the sculpture?

YOKE DANCE Ask students to notice how the two oxen in *Sodbuster* are yoked together. Point out how the oxen would always have to move together. Then, with a partner, have students create some dance moves standing side by side, arm over arm and moving together. Allow some time for experimenting and then have partners perform for the class.

■ GOAL: CREATIVE EXPRESSION

WORK SONG SING-ALONG

Have a sing-along of some favorite work songs. Some good ones to sing are "Erie Canal," "John Henry," and "There's a Hole in the Bucket." After singing the songs, have students make up a verse or two of their own. Then sing the new verses. Students may also enjoy acting out the songs.

■ GOAL: HISTORICAL AND CULTURAL CONTEXT

Oh Boy, Dessert Dances!

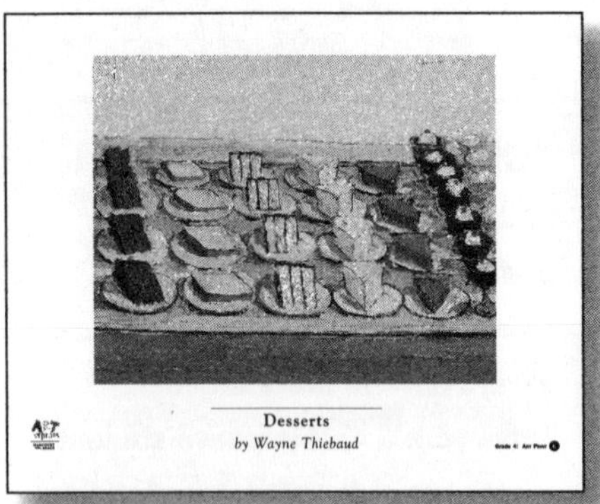

▲ ***Art Print 6,*** *Desserts,* Wayne Thiebaud

OBJECTIVE: Students will create dance movements for a particular kind of dessert, then analyze their own dance as well as the dances of others.

MATERIALS: *Art Print 6, Performing Arts Cassette:* "Emperor's Mare"

TIPS AND TIME-SAVERS

Students may enjoy choosing their own music for their dances. Also, they may want to add sound effects. Encourage their ideas within the bounds of good taste and reason.

WARM-UP

Play "Emperor's Mare" as students view *Desserts*. Ask students to identify the desserts they see in the painting. Discuss the following questions:

- **How do you think the artist feels about dessert? What makes you think that?**
- **What do you notice about the rows of desserts?**

DANCE ACTIVITY

Move the class to an open area. Explain that they are going to move like a dessert. Ask them to name some of the characteristics of pudding. They may say it's sticky, jiggly, fluid, and smooth.

- Now ask students to try to move like pudding. They might want to move in wavy, smooth, or gliding motions.
- After students have experimented on their own, ask the group to form rows of five or six like the puddings they saw in the painting. Guide them through some of the moves you saw them experimenting with. They should try to stay together as they move.
- Now have students form groups of five or six and try to move as their favorite dessert. Remind them of their movements from their "pudding dance." Have them line up in rows and perform again.

Tell students to study the movements of each group and try to guess which dessert the dancers are portraying. They should also watch the dancers to see how they used patterns in their dancing. Then discuss what students observed about the groups, and have them give positive feedback to each other.

REFLECT

Gather students together in front of *Desserts*. Play "Emperor's Mare" as they again study the painting. Then discuss the following:

- **Is there anything in the painting you notice now that you didn't notice before?**
- **Where do you see desserts like these?**
- **The next time you see desserts lined up, what will you be thinking?**

Informal Assessment

✔ What are the characteristics of the best acting/movements?

✔ How did group members work together to learn and experiment with movements?

PATTERNS IN MUSIC Have students march and sing the song "The Grand Old Duke of York." Have them form lines for the marching and movements. When they are finished, discuss the patterns of the song. Let students explore other songs and discover the patterns. Then have them snap their fingers, clap hands, or do another action to emphasize the pattern. ■ GOAL: ARTISTIC PERCEPTION

ACT LIKE A . . . Have students improvise the dialogue between some desserts waiting on the counter. The desserts could make comments to each other about the people who made them and then cut them in pieces, people coming through the line, or the fact that they don't want to be eaten. ■ GOAL: CREATIVE EXPRESSION

Folk Dance Festival

Unit Project Overview: As students study how visual art reflects history and tradition, they research and perform traditional dances.

MATERIALS

- *Performing Arts Cassette*
- commercial or teacher-prepared videotapes of traditional dance performances
- recordings of music for traditional dances
- books about traditional dances from various cultures

VOCABULARY CONCEPTS

You may wish to teach these **Glossary** terms and concepts in context during this project.

folk dance
motif
notation
ritual dance
social dance

CROSS-CURRICULAR CONNECTIONS

Fine Arts Theater, Music, Visual Art
Science Natural Environments
Social Studies Cultural Traditions, History, Geography
Math Geometric Shapes

PROJECT OBJECTIVES

Artistic Perception Respond to themes and ideas expressed in traditional dances from diverse cultures.

Creative Expression Create and perform an original dance based on knowledge of traditional dance forms.

Historical/Cultural Context Research, learn, and perform traditional dances from a variety of cultures.

Aesthetic Valuing Discuss similarities and differences among dances from various cultures.

1 WARM-UP

Choose one of the following activities:

- Have students brainstorm a list of dances that they know how to do or that they know about. Encourage them to include a variety of dances, from contemporary to traditional. Invite volunteers to tell about and demonstrate any such dances they know how to do.
- Have students form groups of four. Play a selection from the *Performing Arts Cassette*. Using four simple moves—step, slide, kick, and turn—have each group make up a repetitive circle dance to the music. As the groups perform for each other, discuss how each group used the movements in different combinations to form dances.

Discuss the following with students. Have them record their responses in their project journals.

- **Think about family or neighborhood celebrations. What dances are performed during these celebrations? Do you join in? Do you enjoy these dances?**
- **What kinds of folk or traditional dances would you like to learn about? Why?**

❷ PLAN THE PROJECT

Set Goals Explain to students that the purpose of the project is to learn about traditional dances and, if they wish, to create their own dance. Assist students in setting project goals:

- learn and perform a dance from your own cultural heritage or from an area of the world in which you are interested
- create a dance about an event or idea important to you

Outline the Project With students, consider

- the scope of the project (see Project Options)
- the audience: Family members? Other classes?
- how to find out about traditional dances from our own cultural backgrounds: From family members? From community groups?
- how to research dances from other cultures and various areas of the world: Community groups? Books? Videos?

Small groups can focus on researching, learning, and performing a particular folk dance. Students can create and perform an original dance based on an event or theme of their choice. All groups can share and teach their dances to other groups.

❸ EXPLORE TRADITIONAL DANCES

- Have students view live performances or videos of traditional dances from a variety of cultures. Resources might include commercial videos, tapes of television programs, and tapes of performances by local dance troupes.
- Ask students to talk with family members about traditional dances from their cultural backgrounds. Suggest that students try to get recordings of music for the dances.
- As students study dances from various parts of the world, have them make a bulletin board display to share other information they learn. In the display, include photographs of students performing dances.

PROJECT OPTIONS

- Have small groups research and learn one dance. Have the groups perform for each other and share the information they learned about the origin of the dance. The groups can teach each other how to do the dances. **SIMPLE**
- Students can create costumes and scenery and perform dances, including original dances, for a special school event. As part of each group's performance, they can give a brief history of the meaning and origin of the dance. After everyone has performed, the groups can teach their dances to audience members. **ELABORATE**

Contact family members, dance troupes, libraries, museums, and historical societies. Invite guests to visit the classroom to talk about and teach traditional dances to students.

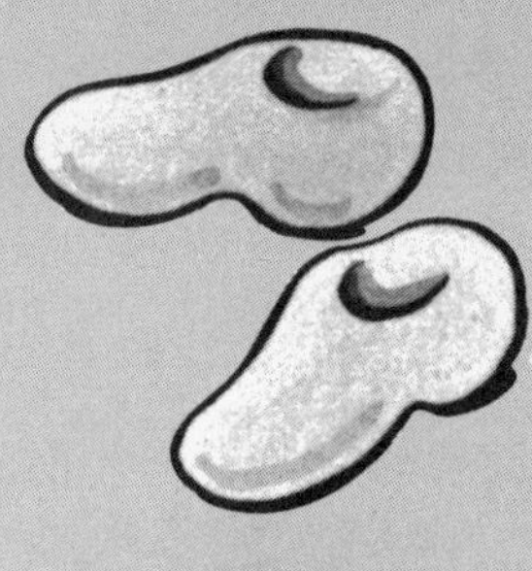

CLASSROOM MANAGEMENT
If possible, arrange for practice sessions to be held in the gym or the cafeteria. For any dance activity, be sure to discuss safety issues and the importance of being aware of other dancers' space.

For Students with Special Needs
Because folk dances usually have a set pattern of movements, students in wheelchairs may not be able to perform dances in the traditional manner. Encourage students to adapt dance movements as necessary to accommodate the needs of all group members.

CAREERS IN ART

Students should be aware of these dance-related careers as they participate in this project.

dance historian
choreographer
folk dancer
costume designer
dance teacher

4 CREATE FOLK DANCE PERFORMANCES

- Help groups identify and organize tasks as necessary.
- Groups who are also creating original dances should decide on a theme and begin creating movements to express the theme. They can use the Copying Master on page 37 as a start.
- If students decide they want to have costumes and/or scenery, they should begin work now.

5 REHEARSE AND REFINE

- Once the groups have learned their dances, hold a rehearsal in which the groups perform for each other. Have the groups tell each other what they have learned about the dances.
- Have groups perform their original dances for each other. Discuss the ideas they are trying to convey.
- If students are going to give a live performance, have at least one dress rehearsal with the groups performing in order.

6 PERFORM IT!

Some options for the performance:
- present the dances live before an audience, and then invite audience members to learn and join in the dances
- videotape the performances to share with family members and community groups

Performance and Process Assessments

Review the project with students. Discuss project journal entries they made over the course of the project. Encourage students to add personal evaluations and responses in their project journals.

✔ For the Student
- What did you learn about dance during this project? Did this project make you want to learn more? About what?
- How did the audience respond to your performance? How did that make you feel?

✔ For the Teacher
- How effectively did students work together to create cohesive dance performances?
- What new insights did students gain about the cultural backgrounds of themselves and others?

Name ______________________

PERFORMING ARTS PROJECT

Folk Dance Festival

Creating Your Own Folk Dance

Folk dances are usually very old. They are passed down from generation to generation. They help people remember and celebrate their culture.

Work with a small group to create your own folk dance. Think of events or ideas that are important to you—things that you want other people to remember and celebrate. Choose one event or idea as the theme for your dance.

Think about these questions as you create your dance:

- What kind of dance should we create? Circle? Line? Square? Partner? Some other kind?
- What movements can we use to express what is important to us?
- What movements do we want to repeat over and over?
- What music will we use? Will we find a piece of recorded music? Will we create our own music with rhythm instruments?
- Will our dance be easy enough for everyone to learn and do?

Maybe the dance you create will be passed on from class to class in your school—just like other folk dances!

Blizzard dance

Room 412 Dance

friendship dance

soccer dance

MUSIC CREATIVE EXPRESSION

Sight and Sound Patterns

▲ ***Art Print 7,*** *Tall Vase,* Maria Martinez

OBJECTIVE: Students translate visual patterns into rhythmic or melodic patterns.

MATERIALS: *Art Print 7, Performing Arts Cassette:* "Dancing with You," percussion instruments, materials for making instruments, electronic keyboard

CLASSROOM MANAGEMENT Set up a sign-up sheet for small groups to use an electronic keyboard or other instrument that may be available for only a short period of time.

WARM-UP

As students look at *Tall Vase,* ask them to imagine what kind of music might be appropriate for it. You may wish to point out that the sculpture was created by a Native American woman. Use the following questions for discussion:

- **What kinds of sounds do you hear when you look at the sculpture?**
- **Would the music for this sculpture be fast or slow?**
- **Notice the patterns in the sculpture. What kinds of ideas do these patterns give you? How do these patterns relate to the music that might go with the sculpture?**

MUSIC ACTIVITY

Using percussion instruments, simple student-made instruments, or an electronic keyboard, have students prepare to study the sculpture and create music to go with it. You may want to guide students through the process with the following questions and suggestions:

- **Let's look at the pattern in the sculpture. First use your hands to trace the pattern in the air.**
- **Now use your musical instruments to create a sound pattern to accompany it. The sound could reflect the long or short lines, the shapes, the height, length, or depth of the lines, or the strength of the images.**
- **Does the sound change in the pattern? How does the sound change?**

Have students experiment with sound patterns in small groups. If possible, group members should use different instruments so they can create simple as well as more complex patterns of music and rhythm.

Have students create a picture for their music patterns. In the picture they should show how each individual instrument is played in the pattern. Encourage them to use color and line to illustrate the music pattern. Allow time for each group to share their picture patterns and music with the whole class.

REFLECT

Display *Tall Vase* again as students discuss the sculpture. Play "Dancing with You" by Lakota George. Ask students to compare and contrast their music pattern with the flute music. Use the following questions for discussion:

- **How does the flute music help you appreciate the sculpture?**
- **How does the music you created help you understand the pattern in the sculpture?**

Informal Assessment

✔ How were students able to observe and attend to patterns in the sculpture and in their music?

✔ How did students respond and participate creatively with their musical creation?

DANCING PATTERNS Have students use "Dancing with You" to create a short dance pattern. When they feel comfortable with the dance steps, have them listen to "Amakonkaguanquichu" from the *Performing Arts Cassette* and try to perform the same dance pattern. Ask them to note how the changes in tempo create variations in the dance pattern. ■ GOAL: CREATIVE EXPRESSION

ORAL INTERPRETATIONS Students may work with favorite short verses or poems to create an oral interpretation. Pairs or small groups may interpret text creatively using a variety of presentation techniques such as echo reading, dramatic reading, repetition, and reading in a round. ■ GOAL: ARTISTIC PERCEPTION

Scenes from Ancient Greece

▲ ***Art Print 8,*** Hydria: *Women Sorting Wool,* Greek vase

OBJECTIVE: Students, guided by the teacher, pantomime the activities shown on the vase in Art Print 8.

MATERIALS: *Art Print 8, Performing Arts Cassette:* "Distribuição de Flôres"

TIPS AND TIME-SAVERS You may want to help students gather some props, such as large bundles of white, beige, or neutral-colored yarn; plastic jars; and wicker baskets, to use as they role-play the scene shown on the vase.

WARM-UP

Have students study *Art Print 8, Hydria: Women Sorting Wool* as you play "Distribuição de Flôres." Ask volunteers to describe the object in *Art Print 8* and what is happening in the scene. Then discuss the following:

- **When does this scene take place? Where? How do you know?**
- **What do you think happened before this scene?**
- **What will happen next?**

THEATER ACTIVITY

Clear a large space in the room. Display *Art Print 8,* and explain that everyone will act out a story about the scene on the vase. Organize students into groups of three, have each group decide who will play which role, and then find a space in the room. Have students pretend to be the people in the scene as you guide them slowly through a story similar to the one below. Encourage them to try to feel and act as the people do in *Art Print 8* and convey these feelings through facial expressions and actions.

- **Imagine that you live in ancient Greece. You wake up in the morning. What do you see? What do you hear? How do you feel?**
- **You go to eat your breakfast with your family. What do you eat? What do you do during breakfast?**
- **Now it's time to do your chores. Today is the day your family shears the sheep. You go outside to where the sheep are kept. What to you do there? How do you work together? What do you see and hear?**
- **This job takes a long time to do. How do you feel when you are finished?**

- **Now it's time to clean the wool. How do you wash it? Where do you get the water? What is each person's job? What do you do first? Next? After that?**
- **Imagine that you are outside, hanging up the wool to dry. How does each person help? What do you see, hear, and smell? How do you feel?**
- **It's the next day and time to spin the wool. How do you do this? Is it hard to do or easy to do?**
- **Now it's time to sort the wool into different batches, and to get it ready for weaving. Have students act out the scene in *Art Print 8* for this step. Now freeze!**

If you want to continue the story from this point, have students work with their groups to brainstorm what would happen next, and then act it out. Allow time for each group to perform for classmates. Remind children that their performance should reflect what they see in Art Print 8.

REFLECT

Ask students to study *Art Print 8* again as you play "Distribuição de Flôres." Then discuss the following:

- **Now that you've acted out scenes from ancient Greece, what do you know about the life of the people shown in *Art Print 8?***
- **How would people today do the same chores?**
- **Why do you think the potter made this vase? Why did the painter paint this scene?**

Informal Assessment

✔ How effectively did students interpret the images on the vase to pantomime a scene?

✔ What understanding did students gain about how a person's culture affects the art he or she creates?

GREEK DANCES Have small groups create dances that incorporate a sequence of movements having to do with preparing wool to be used, such as shearing a sheep, washing the wool, spinning the wool into thread, and weaving. Students may want to use "Distribuição de Flôres" or other selections from the *Performing Arts Cassette* for their dances. Allow time for groups to perform.
■ GOAL: CREATIVE EXPRESSION

MUSIC MATCH Have groups of students listen to selections from the Performing Arts Cassette to find another piece of music that goes well with *Art Print 8.* Display *Art Print 8,* and have each group play its selection for classmates and tell why the piece was chosen.
■ GOAL: AESTHETIC VALUING

Inspiring Songs

Unit Project Overview: As students study the inspirational aspects of visual art, they perform or compose songs about heroes, legendary figures, or important events.

MATERIALS

- *Performing Arts Cassette* and other recordings
- rhythm instruments (optional)
- materials for costumes, scenery, props, visual displays (optional)

VOCABULARY CONCEPTS

You may wish to teach these **Glossary** terms and concepts in context during the project.

beat
call-and-response
contemporary
form
tempo

CROSS-CURRICULAR CONNECTIONS

Fine Arts Theater, Dance, Visual Art
Language Arts Writing, Poetry, Using the Library
Social Studies History, Cultural Traditions

PROJECT OBJECTIVES

Artistic Perception Identify ways in which music can be inspiring.

Creative Expression Choose or compose a song that is in some way inspirational. Perform the song in a theatrical manner to convey particular feelings or ideas.

Historical/Cultural Context Research traditional and folk music for songs about heroes, legends, or events.

Aesthetic Valuing Evaluate and refine performances based on project goals and personal responses.

1 WARM-UP

Choose one of the following activities:

- Have students listen to songs about heroes, legendary figures, or historical events. Include songs from a variety of genres, such as "Casey Jones," "John Henry," "Follow the Drinking Gourd," "Oklahoma," "The Star-Spangled Banner." Encourage responses to the themes and the music. Discuss how the selections make students feel and why.
- Ask students to name songs or musical selections that they find inspiring in some way. If possible, have them bring in recordings to share with the class. Invite volunteers to tell why the music is inspiring; for example, a song might remind them of a family member or friend, or a piece of music might make them feel especially happy.

Discuss the following with students. Have them record responses in their project journals.

- **What kind of music inspires you?**
- **How does the music inspire you? Does it make you feel or act in a certain way?**

❷ PLAN THE PROJECT

Set Goals Explain to students that the purpose of the project is to explore and perform inspiring songs. Assist students with the following:

- learn or compose and perform a song that is inspiring in some way
- embellish the performance with narration, movements, visual displays, or some other theatrical effects

Outline the Project With students, consider

- the scope of the project (see Project Options)
- the audience: Family members? Other classes?
- sources for music: Contemporary songs? Traditional or folk songs? Other kinds of music? Original compositions?
- research needed: When and why was the song written? Who or what is the song about? How can we find out more information about a particular song?

Small groups can be formed based on interest in a particular person, event, or idea. Even if students decide to compose an original song, encourage them to research a variety of music types for models.

❸ EXPLORE INSPIRING MUSICAL IDEAS

- Have students listen and respond to songs and selections representing various music types.
- Show videotapes (or excerpts) of musical theater productions. Discuss how action, costumes, and scenery support and embellish the meaning of songs.
- Encourage students to use their project journals to record information about music they are researching.

PROJECT OPTIONS

- Students can perform their songs for each other with few, if any, theatrical embellishments. Instead, students can discuss why they chose a particular song and share the information they learned about it. **SIMPLE**
- Students can create a formal production, including costumes, scenery, actions, narration, and other such theatrical elements. Performances can be videotaped or performed live for a special school event. **ELABORATE**

CONNECTION

Contact family members or community groups involved in choral singing or in musical theater productions. Invite guests to visit the classroom to coach students about techniques they use to present a song effectively.

❹ CREATE AN INSPIRING PERFORMANCE

- As the groups finalize their song choices, they should begin to memorize the lyrics and learn the melody.
- Groups who are composing original songs might begin with the lyrics and then create the melody. (The Copying Master on page 29 may help them notate the melody.)
- Costumes, scenery, or visual displays for the performances should be worked on.
- Use the Copying Master on page 45 to help students brainstorm performance ideas.

❺ REHEARSE AND REFINE

- Schedule several practice sessions and at least one dress rehearsal with groups performing in order.
- Videotape a rehearsal so students can review and refine their performances.
- If students choose to perform a formal production for an audience, they should send invitations and/or create posters.

❻ PERFORM IT!

Some options for the performance:
- set up an outdoor stage area and perform live before an invited audience
- videotape performances to share with family members, other classes, or community groups

Performance and Process Assessments

Review the project with students. Encourage students to record personal feelings and evaluations in their project journals.

✔ For the Student
- How did you want to inspire the audience? Do you think you succeeded? What makes you think that?
- What was the most surprising thing you learned during this project? Why was it surprising?

✔ For the Teacher
- How did students work cooperatively to produce an effective performance?
- How did students' performances reflect thoughtfulness and creativity?

CLASSROOM MANAGEMENT
Set aside an area of the classroom as the music center. Provide several cassette players and headphone sets. As students research and listen to music, this will avoid confusion and control the noise level.

For Students with Special Needs
All students should be able to participate creatively in project activities. For example, hearing-impaired students (or all students) can use American Sign Language to emphasize song lyrics.

CAREERS IN ART

Students should be aware of the following music-related careers as they work on this project.

historian
lyricist
recording technician
production designer

Name ______________________________

PERFORMING ARTS PROJECT

Inspiring Songs

Telling a Story Through Song

By now you have probably chosen or written an inspiring song. Use this checklist to come up with ideas for performing the song in an inspiring way.

______ Everyone will sing the whole song together.

______ Different group members will sing different parts.

______ We'll sing with a recording of the song.

______ We'll use rhythm instruments to accompany the song.

______ We'll make and wear costumes.

______ We'll make scenery to show what the song is about.

______ We'll provide information about the song for the audience.

______ We'll perform actions or movements to act out the song.

______ We'll use props as we sing.

______ We'll use our voices to show how the song makes us feel.

Use this checklist to make a list of jobs.

THEATER CREATIVE EXPRESSION

The Min and Bill Radio Show

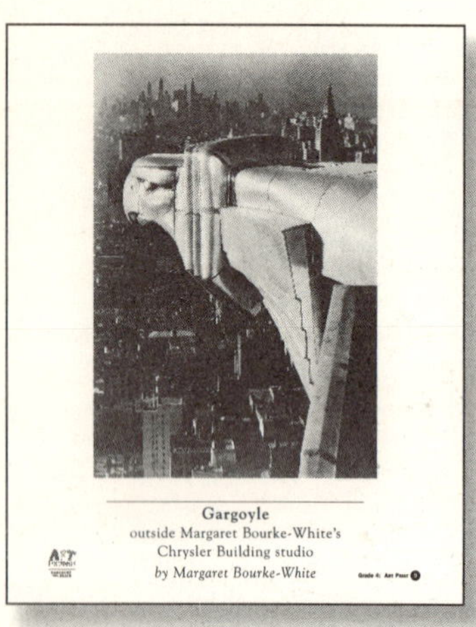

▲ ***Art Print 9,** Gargoyle outside Margaret Bourke-White's Chrysler Building studio,* Margaret Bourke-White

OBJECTIVE: Students create a radio show.

MATERIALS: *Art Print 9, Performing Arts Cassette*: "Allegro Agitato from Piano Concerto in F"

TIPS AND TIME-SAVERS To re-create the old-time radio broadcast feel and help students get into character, have them make a prop resembling a microphone and use it when they present their broadcast. Hats are another device that also help students get into character.

WARM-UP

Set a city mood by playing George Gershwin's "Allegro Agitato from Piano Concerto in F." Display *Art Print 9* and explain what and where it is. Note also that the photographer who took the photograph could see two of these gargoyles from her studio and named them "Min" and "Bill." Then discuss the following questions:

- **What do you think the gargoyle might see from this height?**
- **How do you think the gargoyle might feel about what it sees below it in the city?**
- **If this gargoyle could talk, what would it say?**

THEATER ACTIVITY

Tell students they will be creating a radio show based on what the gargoyles Min and Bill see and report from high above New York City.

- Organize the class into small groups, with each group producing a segment of the radio show.
- Suggest some features for the show such as: "What's New in the City Today," "Interview with the Pigeons," "Who's Visiting," "Big Events" (such as parades for Thanksgiving and St. Patrick's Day), "Traffic," "Emergency," and "Random Acts of Kindness." Students may come up with their own features as well.
- Each group should select a feature to produce and decide who will portray Min and Bill. Additional roles should also be decided and assigned.
- Each group should have a sound-effects person along with a scriptwriter and director.
- Have students create and "broadcast" their portion of the "Min and Bill Show."

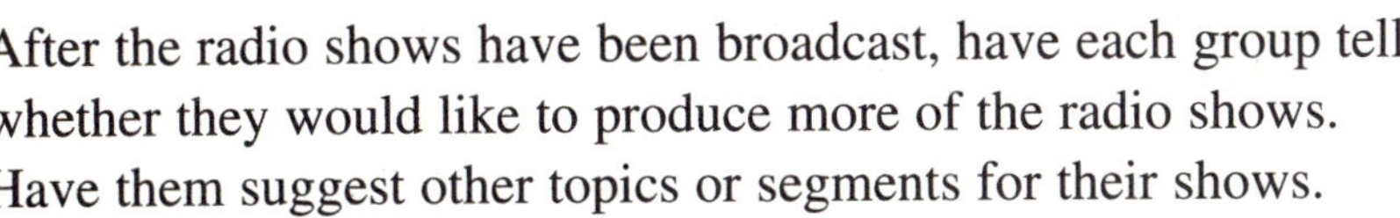

After the radio shows have been broadcast, have each group tell whether they would like to produce more of the radio shows. Have them suggest other topics or segments for their shows.

REFLECT

Gather students in front of *Art Print 9*. Play "Allegro Agitato from Piano Concerto in F" again. Have them absorb the details of the photograph. Then discuss the following questions:

- **Now that you've made the gargoyle into a character, what do you notice in the photograph that you hadn't noticed before?**
- **Would you like to see more of this photographer's work? Why?**

Informal Assessment

✔ Were students able to produce a radio show feature in character?

✔ What new insights into the photograph do students now have?

MAKE A HIT **Have students write the lyrics to a song, or find a song that the gargoyle can sing when it becomes a Broadway star or a singer in a rock band. Then have them perform the song for others the way the gargoyle would sing it. ■ GOAL: CREATIVE EXPRESSION**

GARGOYLE DANCE **Have students practice some simple dance movements to music. Teach them how to freeze in place like a gargoyle when the music stops. Have a camera on hand to capture outstanding freezes. When the photographs have been developed, have students judge them for the most creative or imaginative expressions. ■ GOAL: CREATIVE EXPRESSION/AESTHETIC VALUING**

Temple Building Dance

▲ ***Art Print 10,*** *The Temple of Kukulcan, known as El Castillo (The Castle),* Chichén Itzá, Mexico

OBJECTIVE: Students create a series of dance movements that portray the construction of the temple.

MATERIALS: *Art Print 10, Performing Arts Cassette*: "Amakonkaguanquichu"

CLASSROOM MANAGEMENT
Have students spend additional time, either before or after the dance, finding out more about the people who built this great temple. The World Wide Web offers many sites related to Chichén Itzá and Egypt.

WARM-UP

Display *Art Print 10.* Play "Amakonkaguanquichu" and have students listen especially to the flute and the rhythm. Ask them to close their eyes and imagine that they are one of the temple builders. Then discuss the following questions:

- **Why do you suppose the ancient Mayans wanted to have a temple like El Castillo?**
- **How did the people make this temple?**

DANCE ACTIVITY

Explain to students that they are going to create a dance series that portrays the construction of the temple. Point out that this temple was planned so that at the spring equinox, when the sun sets, the carvings and the stairs look like a moving snake.

Before students begin, make a large construction jobs chart. List the different people who will work on the temple, such as engineers, architects, stonecutters, stonecarvers, stone movers, and others students can think of.

- Once partners or small groups have been organized, students should identify which workers they are going to portray and the movements they wish to include in their dance series.
- Encourage students to be very expressive in their movements. Students should understand that they need to convey the work they are doing through their dance. Also, they should realize that some types of work require more physical strength than others.
- Students should practice their dance first without music and later with music.
- Group three or four small groups or partners together for the performance.

After the groups perform, ask others to tell what they thought each group did well, what they thought was exciting, what would have made the dance better, and what they really liked. Students may enjoy a short session to revisit the dance to make some of the changes that might have been discussed.

REFLECT

Display *Art Print 10* once again. Play "Amakonkaguanquichu" and have students study the work as they listen. Then discuss the following questions:

- **What can you tell about the people who built the temple?**
- **What would you say to them if they were here now?**

Informal Assessment

✔ How were students able to move and convey the occupations they chose?

✔ What insights have students gained regarding El Castillo?

MAYAN BAND Have students create instruments using sticks, several kinds of drums, and simple flutes (students may use recorders, if available), and try replicating the rhythm and music they heard on the cassette or from other Peruvian music that may be available. Have them discuss the qualities of the music. ■ GOAL: HISTORICAL AND CULTURAL CONTEXT

A DAY IN THE LIFE Ask students to think about what a day in the life of a temple worker might have been like. Then have them act out the events of that day. They may do this alone or with a partner. ■ GOAL: HISTORICAL AND CULTURAL CONTEXT

Surprise Endings

Unit Project Overview: As students study how visual artists surprise us with the unexpected in their artworks, they choose or create stories with plot surprises and dramatize them.

MATERIALS

- stories with surprise endings
- videotapes of plays
- materials for costumes and scenery
- materials for creating sound effects

VOCABULARY CONCEPTS

You may wish to teach these **Glossary** terms and concepts in context during the project.

elements of theater
script
stagecraft
storyboard

CROSS-CURRICULAR CONNECTIONS

Fine Arts Music, Dance, Visual Art

Language Arts Writing, Researching Stories with Surprise Endings

Science Lighting, Sound, Fiction Based on Science Themes

Social Studies Traditional Stories, Cultural Traditions

PROJECT OBJECTIVES

Artistic Perception Identify elements in stories and dramatizations that create surprise.

Creative Expression Create and perform a skit or short play with a surprise ending.

Historical/Cultural Context Research traditional tales as a source for story ideas.

Aesthetic Valuing Discuss works-in-progress and revise scripts, staging, scenery, and other elements to produce desired effects.

1 WARM-UP

Choose one of the following activities:

- Read aloud or have students view a dramatization of a story with a surprise ending. Classic stories include "The Gift of the Magi" and "The Ransom of Red Chief" by O. Henry and "The Open Window" by Saki.
- Discuss stories with surprise endings. Ask students to recall stories they have read or seen dramatized that are especially memorable because the endings were unexpected. Encourage volunteers to retell the stories in a dramatic manner so as to surprise the listeners.

Discuss the following with students and have them record their ideas in their project journals.

- **Do you enjoy reading or seeing dramatizations of stories with surprise endings? Why? What is your favorite such story?**
- **If you were to write a story with a surprise ending, would you write about something funny? Scary? Serious? Silly? Why?**

❷ PLAN THE PROJECT

Set Goals Discuss the following project goals with students:

- perform a skit or short play with a surprise ending
- write a script based on an original story or based on a story you have read or seen dramatized
- use costumes, scenery, lighting/sound effects, and other stagecraft to enhance plot surprises

Outline the Project With students, consider:

- the scope of the project (see Project Options)
- the audience: Family members? Other classes? Just ourselves?
- how to come up with story ideas: Create original stories? Research traditional stories? Read library books?

Small groups can be formed based on topic interest.

❸ EXPLORE SURPRISING IDEAS

- Suggest that students consider project goals as they view television programs. Review programming schedules and, if possible, have volunteers videotape teleplays that seem useful as models for their own productions. As students view these videos, including credits, discuss how various dramatic and stagecraft effects were achieved.
- Display and share books such as *Theater Magic: Behind the Scenes at a Children's Theater* by Cheryl Walsh Bellville (Carolrhoda, 1986) and *Behind the Scenes of a Broadway Musical* by Bill Powers (Crown, 1982). See page 64 for additional resources.
- Encourage students to research traditional tales, such as Aesop's fables, for surprising plot ideas. Suggest that they keep track of their research in their project journals by listing stories and by creating idea webs.

PROJECT OPTIONS

- Small groups can perform works-in-progress informally for each other, experimenting with costumes, scenery, lighting/sound effects. Focus on broadening students' awareness and experience of theater as it relates to their personal responses to television and movies. **SIMPLE**
- Have students plan for formal performances with costumes, scenery, and lighting/sound effects. Small groups could perform their skits for an invited audience or for a special school event. Performances could be presented "live" or on videotape. **ELABORATE**

Contact family members or others involved in community theater. Invite guests to visit the classroom for coaching sessions.

CLASSROOM MANAGEMENT

Because of the project theme, it's important that groups work in privacy to ensure the "surprise" aspect of their productions. If possible, schedule practice sessions in areas and/or at times that accommodate this need.

For Students with Special Needs

All students should be able to participate fully and creatively in this project. For example, a hearing-impaired student might incorporate American Sign Language in a plot twist, or a student in a wheelchair might surprise the audience with an unexpected feat.

CAREERS IN ART

Students should be aware of these theater-related careers as they work on this project.

scriptwriter
publicist
set designer
special effects designer

4 CREATE SURPRISING SKITS

- Guide students in creating stories with surprise endings. As they brainstorm plots, ask questions that focus on basic story elements: character, problem/conflict, and resolution.
- Some groups might like to make storyboards to map out the set and actions. Scripts should contain stage directions.
- As the groups finalize their scripts, discuss how they can use stagecraft to enhance their ideas. Use the Copying Master on page 53 to help students focus on costumes, scenery, props, lighting, background music, and sound effects.

5 REHEARSE AND REFINE

- Videotape performances or have groups perform for each other.
- As students consider refinements, have them look critically at the surprise ending.
- If students are going to present formal performances, they should begin sending invitations or creating posters to publicize the event.

6 PERFORM IT!

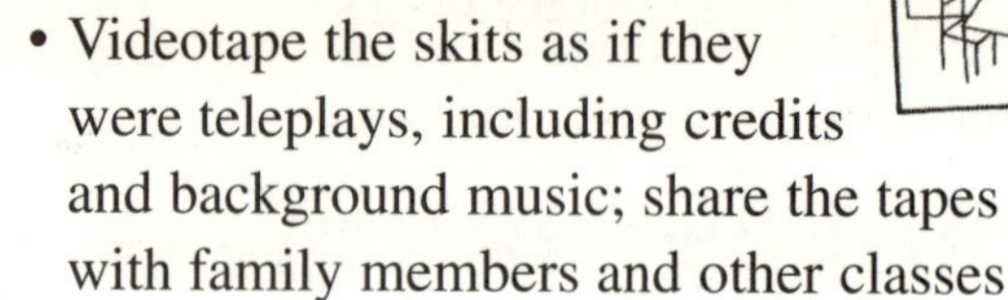

Some options for the performance:

- Videotape the skits as if they were teleplays, including credits and background music; share the tapes with family members and other classes.
- Perform the skits live before an invited audience.

Performance and Process Assessments

Review students' project journal entries and any videotapes or artifacts (such as different versions of scripts or storyboards) that document their progress through the project.

✔ For the Student

- Was this project worth all the work? Why? What was the most enjoyable part of it?
- What part of your group's performance do you think was the most effective or successful? Why do you think that?

✔ For the Teacher

- How did students work together effectively to produce a cohesive performance?
- How did students work creatively to meet project goals?

Name ______________________________

PERFORMING ARTS PROJECT

Surprise Endings

Stagecraft Surprises

The next time you watch a movie or a television show, check the long list of names that comes at the end. Who are all these people?

Now that you are creating your own show, you will discover that writing and acting is only part of the work. Stagecraft is another very important part of putting on a show. As you write your scripts and start acting them out, think about what you would like to do for each of these special areas. Which group members can assist with these areas?

costumes • scenery • props • music • sound effects • lighting effects

DANCE ARTISTIC PERCEPTION

Balanced Movement

▲ ***Art Print 11,*** *Lever No. 3,* Martin Puryear

OBJECTIVE: Students experiment with balance and movement.

MATERIALS: *Art Print 11, Performing Arts Cassette*: "Mobiles"

TIPS AND TIME-SAVERS Have students brainstorm a list of objects and creatures that the sculpture reminds them of.

WARM-UP

Display *Lever No. 3* while playing "Mobiles." Have volunteers describe the sculpture. Discuss the following questions:

- **What does the sculpture remind you of?**
- **What kind of movement is suggested by this sculpture?**
- **What do you think balances the sculpture?**

DANCE ACTIVITY

Have students form groups of no more than four or five. Explain to students that they will be working together to show how different objects or animals move.

- Have students experiment with balance. Ask them to stand on one foot for a short period of time. What do they do to keep from falling over? Do they bend their knee or put their arms out to the side? Ask them to think how they might keep their balance if they had someone on either side of them.
- Have groups think of objects or animals that the sculpture reminds them of. Tell them to use their bodies together to imitate the kinds of movements they believe that animal or object might make.
- Encourage students to pay attention to their fellow group members' movements to help them maintain their balance. It may be helpful if group members join hands or link arms. Ask students to try to keep their movements smooth.

- Have groups practice moving together across the classroom as their object or animal. Each group member should begin moving at the same time. While groups are moving together, call out "stop." Students must hold their poses, trying to maintain their balance.

REFLECT

Have students view *Lever No. 3* once again. Discuss the following questions:

- **What affected your balance during the activity? How did you keep your balance?**
- **What do you notice about the sculpture that you hadn't noticed before?**

Informal Assessment

✔ How did students use balance to represent objects?

✔ How did students collaborate to express their object or animal?

SCULPTURE SKIT **Have students improvise a skit that explains the purpose of the sculpture. Encourage students to think of how the sculpture might be used. Then have them act out some of these uses. ■ GOAL: CREATIVE EXPRESSION**

LEVER MUSIC **Have students listen to "Mobiles" and one other selection from the *Performing Arts Cassette* while viewing *Lever No. 3*. Ask students to listen critically to both pieces of music and decide which piece best fits the sculpture. Have them explain their choice. ■ GOAL: AESTHETIC VALUING**

Musical Collages

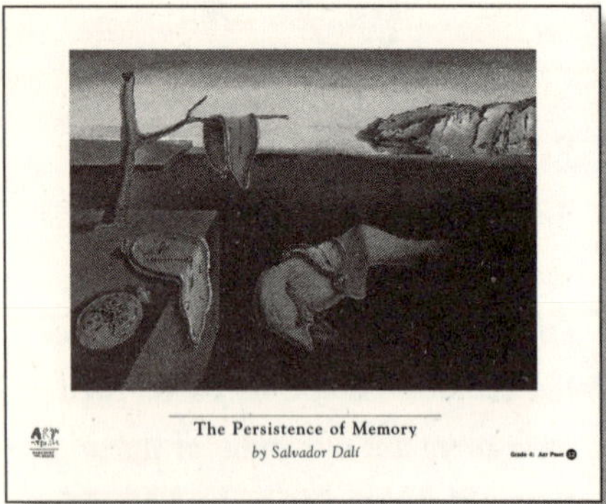

▲ ***Art Print 12,*** *The Persistence of Memory,* Salvador Dalí

OBJECTIVE: Students experiment and create sounds to accompany the painting.

MATERIALS: *Art Print 12, Performing Arts Cassette:* "Opening Parade live at the Bali Arts Festival," tape recorder, found objects for creating sounds

TIPS AND TIME-SAVERS You may wish to have simple instruments available for students to assist them in creating their sound effects.

WARM-UP

Display *The Persistence of Memory* while playing "Opening Parade live at the Bali Arts Festival." Ask volunteers to describe what they see in the painting. Discuss the following questions:

- **What is unusual about the painting?**
- **What does this painting make you think of?**
- **What sounds might you hear if you were in the painting?**

MUSIC ACTIVITY

Explain to students that they will be creating a collage of sound effects to represent the elements in the painting. Have students work in groups to create their own collage of sounds for the painting.

- Have students discuss and identify these elements in the painting: the melting watches, the figure in the foreground, the dead tree, the mountains in the background, the table, the pocket watch, the ants, and the squared sea.
- Ask students to think about what kinds of sounds these objects might make. How does a melting watch's tick sound? What do scurrying ants sound like? Ask students how they might create these sounds.
- Encourage students to experiment with different objects to create sounds representing the elements in the painting. Have them use objects they find around the classroom or school grounds as well as some simple musical instruments.

- Once groups have created their sounds, have them play them all together to hear how they sound. Have groups experiment with different combinations of sounds. When each group creates a collage of sounds they like, have them record the finished collage.

Have each group play their musical collages for their classmates. Encourage students to discuss them with the following questions:

- **Is the music a good representation of the unusual objects in the painting?**
- **Can you identify specific objects with individual sounds in the music?**

REFLECT

Have students study *The Persistence of Memory* once again. Discuss the following questions:

- **What part of the painting is the most difficult to represent with sound? Why?**
- **What questions would you like to ask Salvador Dalí?**

Informal Assessment

✔ How did students use sound to bring the painting to life?

✔ How did the music give students new insights into the painting?

MEMORY DANCE Have students listen to "Opening Parade live at the Bali Arts Festival" from the *Performing Arts Cassette*. Ask students to create an expressive dance that reminds them of the elements in the painting. Encourage them to find other pieces of music to accompany their dances. ■ GOAL: CREATIVE EXPRESSION

SURREAL THEATER Have students act out the painting. Have them start by pantomiming the objects in the painting. For example, some students can be the melting watches; others can be the ants on the watch. Encourage students to try to be other inanimate objects, such as the table and the tree. ■ GOAL: CREATIVE EXPRESSION

Name ______________________________

Group/Self-Assessment for Unit Projects

Answer the questions below to help you evaluate your work.

1. What do you like best about your performance? Explain.

____

____

____

____

____

2. What is your biggest challenge in creating your performance?

____

____

____

____

____

3. What will you change about your performance when you rehearse it next?

____

____

____

____

____

Name ______________________________

Peer Assessment for Unit Projects

Answer the questions below to evaluate your classmates' performance.

1. Did you enjoy the performance? Explain why or why not.

____

____

____

____

____

2. Did the performers work well together? Explain.

____

____

____

____

____

3. How did the performers create interest for the audience?

____

____

____

____

____

Glossary of Performing Arts Terms

ACTING The process by which an individual uses his or her body, mind, voice, and emotions to interpret the role of a character.

ACTION The sense of forward movement created by the events of a play and the motivations of its characters.

ACTOR A person who acts the part of a character in a play.

AUDIENCE Any person or group watching or listening to a performance, viewing art, or reading a written work.

AXIAL MOVEMENT Movement of body parts around the axis of the body—for example, twisting, reaching, and pivoting—which is anchored to one spot.

BACKSTAGE The area offstage that includes the dressing rooms and storage places for props and scenery.

BALLET A classical dance form that originated in the Renaissance courts of Europe. Steps and body positions were set in the 1600s. The Romantic ballet, as it is known today, began in the 1800s, led by Jules Perrot in France, August Bournonville in Denmark, and Marius Petipa in Russia. Further development was the work of Michel Fokine (Russia); Kenneth MacMillan and Anthony Tudor (England); and George Balanchine, Jerome Robbins, and Arthur Mitchell (United States).

BAND A group of musicians who play instruments together.

BAROQUE MUSIC An exuberant and emotional style of music that was developed in Europe between about 1600 and 1750. It is exemplified in the operas of Claudio Monteverdi and in the concertos of Johann Sebastian Bach and Antonio Vivaldi.

BEAT The basic unit of time in music.

BLOCKING, STAGING The positions (center stage, downstage, upstage, stage right, stage left) and movements of the actors on the stage that are designed to focus the audience's attention on the important points of action.

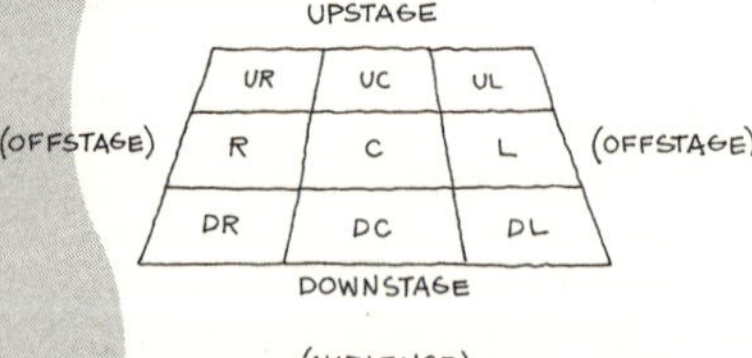

BRASS FAMILY A group of metal instruments, such as the trumpet, that are blown into.

CALL-AND-RESPONSE A musical form in which one performer is echoed or answered by another or by a group. This also occurs with dance movements. It is associated with African music and dance.

CAST All of the actors in a performance.

CHARACTER A person in a play whose physical, mental, and emotional characteristics are portrayed by an actor.

CHORD A combination of three or more tones sounded at once.

CHOREOGRAPHER A person who composes dances.

CHOREOGRAPHY The art of composing dances.

CLASSICAL MUSIC **1.** Art music of any culture, as distinguished from folk or popular music or jazz. **2.** European music of the classical period, from about 1750 to 1825, for example, music by Haydn, Mozart, and Beethoven.

CONFLICT The problem that sets up the action and must be resolved by the end of the play.

CONTEMPORARY Music or other art marked by characteristics of the present period.

COSTUME Clothing worn by a performer to enhance interpretation of his or her character.

CREATIVE DRAMA An improvisation in which participants are guided by a leader to imagine a situation and react to it.

CREATIVE MOVEMENT, CREATIVE DANCE, OR MOVEMENT EXPLORATION Dance based on improvisation, usually to express an emotion, a theme, or a movement element such as time, force, or space.

DANCE **1.** A work of movement that is unified in the manner of a poem, a piece of music, a play, or a painting. It has structure and a purpose or a set of movement themes. It is often accompanied by music. **2.** The field of study of expressive movement and its place in society in the past and present. It includes methods of choreography and performance and other related studies.

DANCE NOTATION A system of recording dance movements. Best known are Benesh notation and Laban notation; however, recent technology has made videotape the most popular method of recording dance.

DANCE STYLE **1.** An individual performer's way of performing any kind of dance. **2.** A particular dance technique, such as that taught at the Vaganova Choreographic Institute in Russia; a historical period of dance, such as Romantic ballet (1880s) or early modern dance (1900 to 1940).

DANCE TYPE (GENRE) Genres include ballet, modern, tap, jazz, Indonesian, and East Indian. Each kind of dance has its own technique, system, vocabulary, form, and method of performance.

DIALOGUE The words spoken by actors as the speech of their characters.

DIRECTOR The director of a performance who coordinates all aspects of the production.

DRAMA **1.** A play written to be performed by actors. **2.** The study of writing and performing plays.

DYNAMICS **1.** The volume of sound. **2.** The marks used to indicate how loudly or softly music is to be performed.

ELEMENTS OF DANCE The components used to create dance. These components are *force/energy, space,* and *time.*

ELEMENTS OF MUSIC The components used to create works of music. These components are *dynamics, form, harmony, pitch, rhythm, tempo, texture,* and *timbre.*

ELEMENTS OF THEATER The components used to create works of theater. These components are *character, dialogue, plot,* and *theme.*

ENSEMBLE A group of performers able to work together to present a production.

ENTERTAINMENT OR COMMERCIAL DANCE An American type of dance—often employing jazz, tap, ballet, and modern dance—used in Broadway musicals, film, television, and music videos.

EXPRESSION A quality of a composition or performance that produces an emotional effect.

FOLK DANCE Dance connected with a country's traditions.

FOLK MUSIC, FOLK SONG Traditional music that has been passed from generation to generation.

FORCE/ENERGY This dance element involves the release of potential energy into kinetic energy. Body weight and gravity affect the motion of the dancers through space.

FORM The structure of a piece of music, achieved through the use of techniques such as repetition, contrast, unity, and variety to organize musical ideas.

FORMAL PRODUCTION The staging of a theatrical work for presentation for an audience. It also refers to music and dance.

GREEK THEATER The term usually refers to the style of theater of ancient Greece, developed in the fifth century B.C.

HARMONY The blending of two or more tones sounded simultaneously; a progression of chords.

IMPROVISATION The spontaneous creation of movement, music, or a character or scene.

INFORMAL PRODUCTION The exploration of a theatrical work in a setting geared to experimentation. It also refers to music and dance.

INSTRUMENT A device used to produce musical sounds, such as a violin or a saxophone.

JAZZ A style of music that originated in the American South with African Americans; it has strong rhythm, improvisation, and syncopation. Influential jazz musicians include Scott Joplin, Louis Armstrong, Duke Ellington, and Billie Holiday.

JAZZ DANCE Dance characterized by movement isolations and complex rhythms. Jazz dance grew from the music of African American ragtime, jazz, spirituals, blues, and work songs. Its rhythms and gestures also show East Indian, gypsy, Spanish, Caribbean, and South American influences.

KINESTHETIC AWARENESS Conscious perception of movement. Kinesthetic awareness is fostered in dance education.

LOCOMOTOR MOVEMENT The movement of the body through space. It may be described by type of movement, such as *walk, run, leap,* or *skip*.

MELODY A succession of musical tones in a rhythmic pattern.

MIDI (Musical Instrument Digital Interface) A standardized "language" that allows electronic instruments to communicate with one another and with a computer.

MODERN DANCE A twentieth-century dance genre that began by breaking away from the formal steps and positions of ballet to produce a more expressive movement. It was first explored by American Isadora Duncan in Europe and by Mary Wigman and Rudolph Laban in Germany. Innovators in the United States were Ruth St. Denis, Ted Shawn, Martha Graham, Doris Humphrey, and Charles Weidman.

MONOLOGUE A dramatic sketch performed by one person.

MOTIF A distinctive gesture used at recurring intervals to unify dance ideas.

NARRATOR Someone who tells a story or outlines a presentation or play for an audience.

NOTATION The methods used to record music, dance, or directions for staged productions.

ORCHESTRA A large group of musicians playing together, usually for a formal presentation.

PANTOMIME Using movement and gesture to convey an idea, an emotion, or a character without using the voice.

PERCUSSION FAMILY A group of instruments, such as drums, that are struck or shaken.

PERFORMANCE MEDIA Media via which stories can be presented. They may include stage, film or videotape, television, radio, audio recording, and computer.

PHRASE A music or dance idea comparable to a sentence or a phrase in language.

PITCH The highness or lowness of a sound, determined by the frequency of the vibration producing it.

PLAY A story that is acted out for an audience. The characters' parts are written in script form for actors to follow.

PLOT The sequence of events that tells what happens in a play. It includes the problem the characters face, how they work to solve it, and how the problem is resolved.

POPULAR DANCE Contemporary dance prevalent at a particular time, for example, the jitterbug, the twist, or hip-hop.

POSTMODERN DANCE A type of dance introduced by Merce Cunningham that emerged in the 1960s. The use of pedestrian gesture and minimalism is characteristic of this type of dance; it is exemplified by Yvonne Ranier, Trisha Brown, Steve Paxton, and Rudy Perez.

PROP, PROPERTY Any object used to help make the character or setting believable.

RHYTHM An organized pattern of pulses or beats. It may be regular or irregular and may involve music or simply sounds made by the human body, such as foot stomps, heartbeats, or breath.

RITUAL DANCE A type of dance connected with the religious or traditional ceremonies of a particular culture.

ROLE The part of a character in a play. It is written by the playwright and interpreted by the actor.

ROLE PLAYING Improvising action and dialogue to portray a given situation, for example, a telephone conversation.

ROUND A melody started at different times by two or more musicians, who sing or play it together. This term can also refer to dance.

SCENE **1.** A short incident that is part of a longer play. **2.** The location of the action.

SCENERY Backdrops and furnishings that create for the audience the setting of the play's story.

SCRIPT The written dialogue, description, and directions for a play.

SET The physical setting, created by scenery and furniture, for the action of a play.

SETTING The time and place of the action of the play.

SHADOW PLAY, SHADOW DANCE A drama in which actors perform with a light source behind them and a screen (possibly a bedsheet) in front of them, so that the audience sees only their silhouettes on the screen.

SHAPE An aspect of space that involves the line of the body, affecting movement. Shape can be symmetrical or asymmetrical, open or closed, jagged or smooth.

SOCIAL DANCE A dance usually done with others in a social setting, such as ballroom dancing and square dancing.

SOUND EFFECTS Sound that imitates something real in a presentation, such as a play, a radio show, or a movie.

SPACE As an element of dance, the space surrounding the body in all directions. The use of space includes shape, direction, path, range, and level of movement.

STAFF A set of five horizontal lines on and around which musical notes are written.

STAGE Any place used for presenting shows to an audience.

STAGECRAFT The knowledge and skills required to handle the physical aspects of a production, such as scenery, props, lights, and sound.

STORYBOARD A graphic, visual outline of the sequence of events in a performance, such as an improvisation, a play, a film, or a television drama.

STORYTELLER A person who passes on a story by oral tradition; a person who dramatically tells a story rather than reading it.

STRING FAMILY A group of instruments, such as the violin, that are played by rubbing a bow against strings.

SYNCOPATION The temporary displacement of the regular beat.

TAP DANCE A type of dance based on rhythmic footwork, with roots in African American dance and Irish and English clogging traditions. Some leading performers and choreographers of tap dancing have been Bill "Bojangles" Robinson, Gregory Hines, Fred Astaire, and Gene Kelly.

TECHNIQUE The skills an artist must acquire for performing.

TEMPO The rate of speed of the music, based on the beat.

TEXTURE A pattern of musical sound created by tones or lines played or sung together. The thickness or thinness of sound is determined by the number of voices or instruments heard at one time.

THEATER Art that is focused toward the formal presentation of a scripted play. It includes acting, directing, designing, managing, and other technical tasks.

THEME The idea that is the focus of a composition.

TIMBRE The quality of tone produced by a particular voice or instrument.

TIME An element of dance involving rhythm, phrasing, tempo, accent, and duration. Time can be measured by music.

TONE **1.** A particular pitch. **2.** A musical note. **3.** The quality of a sound. **4.** The timbre of a particular instrument or voice.

VISUALIZATION A mental image of something that one creates in the mind's eye.

WOODWIND FAMILY A group of wind instruments, such as the clarinet and the flute, on which sound is produced by vibrating one or two reeds in the mouthpiece or by the passing of air over a mouth hole.

Cross-Curricular Connections

	Reading/ Literature	Language Arts/Writing	Social Studies
PERFORMING ARTS PROJECTS			
DANCE **Unit 1:** Nature Dance	✔	✔	✔
THEATER **Unit 2:** Monologues in Character	✔	✔	✔
MUSIC **Unit 3:** Musical Collages		✔	✔
DANCE **Unit 4:** Folk Dance Festival			✔
MUSIC **Unit 5:** Inspiring Songs		✔	✔
THEATER **Unit 6:** Surprise Endings	✔	✔	
ART PRINT/PERFORMING ARTS ACTIVITIES			
THEATER *Art Print 1: Hunt's Vase* A Dialogue: "At Home with..."	✔	✔	
MUSIC *Art Print 2: Still Life* Music for a Meal			✔
DANCE *Art Print 3: The Gourmet* Dinner Dance			✔
MUSIC *Art Print 4: The Boating Party* Colorful Music Creations		✔	✔
THEATER *Art Print 5: Sodbuster: San Isidro* Portrait of Farm Life		✔	✔
DANCE *Art Print 6: Desserts* Oh Boy, Dessert Dances!			
MUSIC *Art Print 7: Tall Vase* Sight and Sound Patterns	✔		
THEATER *Art Print 8: Hydria: Women Sorting Wool* Scenes from Ancient Greece			
THEATER *Art Print 9: Gargoyle outside Margaret Bourke-White's Chrysler Building studio* The Min and Bill Radio Show		✔	✔
DANCE *Art Print 10: The Temple of Kukulcan known as El Castillo (The Castle)* The Temple Building Dance			✔
DANCE *Art Print 11: Lever No. 3* Balanced Movement			
MUSIC *Art Print 12: The Persistence of Memory* Musical Collages			

Science	Math	Fine Arts	Health/Physical Education
PERFORMING ARTS PROJECTS			
✔		✔	✔
		✔	
✔	✔	✔	
✔	✔	✔	✔
		✔	
ART PRINT/PERFORMING ARTS ACTIVITIES			
		✔	
		✔	
		✔	✔
		✔	✔
		✔	
	✔	✔	✔
✔		✔	✔
		✔	
		✔	
	✔	✔	✔
		✔	✔
		✔	✔

Resources for the Performing Arts

BOOKS

Acting & Theatre by Cheryl Evans and Lucy Smith. EDC Publishing, 1992.

Drama for Learning by Dorothy Heathcote and Gavin Bolton. Heinemann, 1995.

Ella Jenkins' This Is Rhythm by Ella Jenkins. Sing Out Corporation, 1993.

The Good Apple Guide to Creative Drama by Kathy U. Foley, Mara Lud, Carol Power. Good Apple, 1981.

Great Composers by Piero Ventura. G.P. Putnam's Sons, 1988.

A Handbook of Creative Dance and Drama by Alison Lee. Heinemann, 1985.

Hands Around the World: 365 Ways to Build Cultural Awareness & Global Respect by Susan Milord. Williamson Publishing, 1992.

The Incredible Indoor Games Book by Bob Gregson. Fearon, 1982.

International Playtime by Wayne E. Nelson and Henry Glass. Fearon, 1992.

Jazz: History, Instruments, Musicians, Recordings by John Fordham. Dorling Kindersley, 1993.

Kids Make Music by Avery Hart and Paul Mantell. Williamson Publishing, 1993.

Making Music: Six Instruments You Can Create by Eddie Herschel Oates. HarperCollins, 1995.

Open Ears: Musical Adventures for a New Generation, edited by Sara deBeer. Ellipsis Kids..., 1995.

Putting on a Play: A Guide to Writing and Producing Neighborhood Drama by Susan and Stephen Judy. Scribner's, 1982.

Theater Games for the Classroom by Viola Spolin. Northwestern University Press, 1986.

We All Go Together: Creative Activities for Children to Use with Multicultural Folksongs by Doug Lipman. Oryx Press, 1994.

The Young People's Book of Music by Keith Spence. Millbrook. Aladdin Books, 1993.

INTERNET

ArtsEdge: The National Arts and Information Network: http://artsedge.kennedycenter.org/artsedge.html

Heinemann Arts Subject Guide: http://www.reedbooks.com.au/heinemann/subject/art.html

The Improv Page: http://sunee.uwaterloo.ca/~broehl/improv/index.html

Marsalis on Music: http://www.wnet.org.mom/index.html

STOMP: http://www.usinteractive.com/stomp/home.html

Yahooligans Art Soup: http://www.yahooligans.com/Art_Soup/

Dr. T's Sing-Along CD (Scholastic) Grades 1-5 (MAC/WIN CD)

Hollywood (Theatrix Interactive) Grade 4 up (MAC/WIN CD)

Julliard Music Adventure (Theatrix Interactive) Grade 4 up (MAC/WIN CD)

Kid Riffs CD (IBM Software) Grade 2 up (WIN CD)

Lamb Chop Loves Music CD (Phillips Media Software) Grades 1-3 (MAC/WIN CD)

Making Music CD (Voyager) Grade 2 up (MAC/WIN CD)

Microsoft Musical Instruments CD (Microsoft) Grade 4 up (MAC/WIN CD)

Opening Night CD (MECC) Grades 3-12 (MAC/WIN CD)

Thinkin' Things, Collections 1, 2, & 3 Grades PreK–8 Edmark (MAC/WIN CD)

Creative Movement: A Step Towards Intelligence (1993, Kultur)

Classic Composers Series (1987, Telemusic)

Kids Make Music (1994, Music Rhapsody)

Leonard Bernstein's Young People's Concerts (1990, Video Music)

Video Dictionary of Classical Ballet (1983, Kultur)